A Beginner's Guide to Salah

KISA PUBLICATIONS
Under the guidance of Moulana Nabi R Mir (Abidi)

For audio recordings of all the parts of prayer,
scan the QR code or visit:

https://kisakids.org/pages/salah-recordings

Photos: Freepik.com, Pixabay.com, ImamHussain.org

Layout and Design by Irum Abbas

Disclaimer: Religious texts have ***not*** been translated verbatim so as to meet the developmental and comprehension needs of children.

Library of Congress Control Number: 2022921694

For permission requests, please write to the publisher at the address below.

Kisa Publications
4415 Fortran Court
San Jose, CA 95134
www.alkisafoundation.org
info@alkisafoundation.org

Dedication

Dedicated to those who sacrificed their lives to protect ṣalāh and to the beloved Imām of our time (ʿaj). May Allah (swt) hasten his appearance so that he may lead our ṣalāh.

Acknowledgments

"On the Day of Resurrection, the ink of the scholars will be weighed up against the blood of the martyrs, and the ink of the scholars will be heavier than the blood of the martyrs."

PROPHET MUḤAMMAD (ṣ)
(NAHJ AL-FAṢĀḤAH, SAYING #3222)

True reward lies with Allah (swt), but we would like to sincerely thank Brother Ali Aqib Jaffry and Sisters Sabika Mithani, Naseem Rangwala, Fatima Hussain, Nida Syed, and Fatemah Karim. May Allah (swt) bless them in this world and the next.

Marḥūmīn Dedication

We humbly request our readers to pray for the health and long life of the parents and recite a Fātiḥah for the marḥūmīn of our team members who diligently worked toward this booklet, especially for the families of Ali Aqib Jaffry, Syed Misbah ur Raza Naqvi and Marḥūm Syed Akhter Ali Moosavi, Marḥūm Munawar Ali Abbas, Marḥūm Mirza Khuda Quli Baig (Aijaz), Marḥūm Sadiq Mithani, Marḥūma Muslima Khatoon, and Marḥūma Munawwar Bano.

Transliteration Chart

Arabic terms in this booklet have been transliterated according to the following guidelines:*

ء	a, i, or u (initial form)	ص	ṣ
ء	ʾ(medial or final form)	ض	ḍ
ا	a	ط	ṭ
ب	b	ظ	ẓ
ت	t	ع	ʿ
ث	th	غ	gh
ج	j	ف	f
ح	ḥ	ق	q
خ	kh	ك	k
د	d	ل	l
ذ	dh	م	m
ر	r	ن	n
ز	z	ه	h
س	s	و	w
ش	sh	ي	y

ـَ	a	آ / ـَا / ىٰ	ā
ـِ	i	ـِي	ī
ـُ	u	ـُو	ū
ـّ	double letter		

*Please note that due to limitations, the transliteration is not 100% accurate in capturing tajwīd rules.

Imām al-Bāqir (ʿa):

الصَّلَاةُ عَمُودُ الدِّينِ

Prayer is the pillar of religion.

Preface

Ṣalāh (prayer) is a gateway to Allah and the pillar of Islam. Through prayer, we can establish a strong connection with Allah. We must realize that when we are standing for prayer, we are standing in front of our Creator, the Lord of the Worlds. When we utter the words Bismillāh, we are speaking to our Nurturer. Reflecting on this will help us achieve greater focus and clarity when we are praying.

Spirituality and building a connection is a gradual process that builds over time. Sometimes, we may feel as though our spiritual connection is not present; however, this is something that will build over time and with effort. The fact that five times a day, we stop everything we are doing and dedicate time to speak with our Creator gives organization and order to our lives. We are moving away from our hectic schedules to a set schedule in which we are in a state of tranquility as we converse with our Nurturer. This is the true beauty of ṣalāh.

Of course, we can speak to Allah in any manner we wish, but our Creator has mandated ṣalāh as a means of conversing with him, as He knows this is the best way we can connect with Him. Many individuals wonder, why are there so many specific procedures for ṣalāh? Āyatullāh Bahjat has a beautiful answer to this question. He explains that when you want to reach a close destination, you can walk there. There is not much danger in walking; therefore, there are very few rules for pedestrians. If the destination is a little further, you may use a bicycle to get there. Since the speed of a bicycle is greater than walking, bikers have more laws. If the distance increases more, one will need a car to reach the destination. Since driving a car is much quicker and has the potential to be more dangerous, there are many more regulations for drivers. However, if one needs to cross the ocean, he or she would need to fly in an airplane. Again, airplanes fly much quicker, so the potential for danger increases with this vessel, hence the significantly greater rules for pilots. Now, when one wants to go into outer space, they will need a space shuttle to get there. As we all know, there are a plethora of regulations for astronauts when operating a rocketship. From this pattern, we see that as our speed of travel increases, the potential for danger increases, and so we need to be more careful and have more rules and regulations in place for our safety.

So, imagine that when you are performing a two rakaʿāt ṣalāh, this is the miʿrāj of the believer — a direct ascension to Allah. It only makes sense that as we are embarking on this great journey to the Highest of the High, we must prepare ourselves in the best of ways and ensure that we are abiding by the guidelines! This is why there are so many aḥkām (Islamic rulings) for ṣalāh — they are in place to ensure that reach our lofty destination safely, inshāʾAllah!

Allah, through His divine mercy, has gifted us this ṣalāh to reach higher levels of spirituality and become closer to Him. In order to preserve this sacred connection, these aḥkām will help us reach these goals.

We pray that this booklet will serve as a beneficial means for you to learn the correct method and philosophy of ṣalāh.

With Duʿās,

Nabi R. Mir (Abidi)

About the Board ʿĀlim

Moulana Nabi R. Mir (Abidi) is a scholar, an educator, a father, and an enthusiast for creating educational infrastructure and Islamic resources for the benefit of the global community. Always wanting to think 'outside of the box' by supporting the creation of innovative materials to engage young readers to pick up Islamic books, interact with Qurʾānic games, learn from the Steps to Perfection Curriculum, and begin their life-long journey of holistic education.

Being a dedicated student and graduate of *Darse Khārij* from the *Ḥawzah* (the Highest Level of Islamic Studies in the Seminary), Moulana Abidi knows the value of Islamic education. Also, having grown up in India, and now residing in the United States, he has had the honor of traveling to various communities and meeting many community leaders. He values the importance of collaboration and working together to optimize potentials, and to create open source platforms so that information and resources are available and accessible to everyone around the world.

You, dear reader, are now part of the Al-Kisa family.
Share the word, and join the mission.

Table of Contents

“

The first thing that Allah
made obligatory
upon my ummah
were the five prayers;

and the first thing from their
acts of worship that
shall be taken up
will be the five prayers;

and the first thing that they will
be questioned about
will be the five prayers.

-Prophet Muḥammad (ṣ) (*Kanz al-ʿUmmāl*, Vol. 7, Ḥadīth #18859)

”

Why Ṣalāh?

"And I have not created the jinn and the men except that they should worship Me." (51:56)

The root word of 'ṣalāh' in Arabic means "connection" or "communication." Ṣalāh (prayer) is the pillar of Islam, without which our faith cannot be kept strong. While there are different ways of speaking to Allah, He has specifically asked us to communicate with Him through ṣalāh. It is our check-in, five times a day, that allows us to thank Allah (swt) and reassess our day to ensure that we're working towards our ultimate purpose in life. In Islam, there are two main kinds of wājib (required) ṣalāh: the occasional prayers and daily prayers.

The occasional prayers include:
- Ṣalāt al-Mayyit (Prayer for the Deceased)
- Ṣalāt al-Āyāt (Prayer for the Signs)*
- Ṣalāt aṭ-Ṭawāf (Prayer after circumambulating the Kaʿbah)
- One's own qaḍā (late) prayers
- Qaḍā (late) prayers of the deceased father on the son

The five daily prayers are known as:
- Fajr (2 rakaʿāt)
- Ẓuhr (4 rakaʿāt)
- ʿAṣr (4 rakaʿāt)
- Maghrib (3 rakaʿāt)
- ʿIshāʾ (4 rakaʿāt)

Please refer to official prayer timing websites for exact timings based on your location

The daily prayers are the focus of this book. Designed for beginners, this booklet will explore the meaning, benefits, and method of ṣalāh with some illustrations to enhance understanding. We pray this booklet will be useful to those who hope to learn not only how to pray, but also to understand the meaning behind the actions we perform during ṣalāh.

*To be read during some natural disasters (e.g., lunar/solar eclipses, earthquakes and thunderstorms).

Conditions of Ṣalāh

There are certain conditions that must be met before a person can pray:

- One should know that the time of prayer has arrived.
- The prayer clothes must be *ṭāhir* (clean/removed from impurities).

  For men, the prayer dress must cover at the very least their private parts, although it is highly recommended to be covered from the navel to the knee.

  Women must cover their body completely, with the exception of their face, hands (up to the wrist), and feet (up to ankles). In the presence of non-*maḥram* men, the feet must be covered as well.
- One should be in a state of *wuḍūʾ* (ritual purification/ablution).
- The space for ṣalāh shouldn't be *ghasbī* (usurped). Seek permission to offer prayers if you aren't in your home, a masjid, or a public place.
- One must face the direction of the *qiblah* (the Kaʿbah in Mecca).

On a basic level, ṣalāh is accepted when its external actions and rules

are applied properly. A higher level of acceptance happens when the individual forms a connection with Allah (swt) that reforms the person, keeping him/her away from sins and improves his/her *akhlāq* (behavior). As you perform the following physical actions, aim to achieve that higher level of spiritual connection.

Benefits of Ṣalāh

Ṣalāh was prescribed for our benefit. It:

Reminds us of Allah, increases our love and bond with Him

Helps us deal with difficult moments in our lives

Keeps us away from bad choices, thoughts, or temptations

Brings discipline to our lives

Keeps our spiritual progress in check throughout the day

Opens the doors of Allah's mercy to us

Wuḍūʾ

"O you who believe! When you stand up for prayer, wash your face and hands up to the elbows, and wipe a part of your head and your feet up to the ankles." (5:6)

Introduction & Benefits of Wuḍūʾ

Spiritual cleanliness is an important part of Islam. It is recommended to be in a state of ṭahārah (purity) while performing acts of worship; however, certain acts require further spiritual cleanliness, such as ṣalāh, which requires the worshipper to be in a state of wuḍūʾ. In Islam, wuḍūʾ, the minor ablution, is a ritual act of worship that should be done with the intention of seeking nearness of Allah.

Just as a shield protects our physical bodies, wuḍūʾ is a spiritual shield that protects our souls. If we perform our wuḍūʾ with concentration, and pay attention to its actions and their significance, this will help us become closer to Allah and improve our concentration in ṣalāh, inshāʾAllāh.

The Noble Prophet (ṣ) has said:

On the Day of Judgment, the believers will be identified through traces on their faces. When someone asked what these traces are, he replied, "The light from having done wuḍūʾ."

(*Biḥār al-Anwār*, Vol. 77, Ḥadīth # 11)

It is mustaḥab to always be in the state of wuḍūʾ. Even performing ordinary actions in a state of wuḍūʾ adds *barakah* (blessings) to those actions. In fact, if one sleeps in the state of wuḍū, they receive the reward of having worshipped the entire night. The Noble Prophet (ṣ) has said, "When one sleeps in a state of wuḍūʾ, their bed becomes a masjid and their sleep is as though they are receiving the reward of performing ṣalāh all night until the morning."[1]

Philosophy of Wuḍūʾ

Prophet Muḥammad (ṣ) has described the symbolic significance of wuḍūʾ as follows:

When we wash our faces, we are washing away the sins that our eyes and mouths have committed. When we wash our arms and hands, we are washing away the sins that our arms and hands have committed. And when we wipe our feet, we are wiping the sins that our feet have committed by taking us to places where we committed sins.[2]

It is important to note that merely performing wuḍūʾ will not wipe away our sins. Rather, this ḥadīth is stating that if we are sincere in our repentance from sins, especially during wuḍūʾ, then we can be hopeful that Allah will eradicate the sins that were facilitated by those body parts. Moving forward, we should be careful not to use those same body parts to perform additional sins.

In the following duʿās, we see the philosophy for each of the steps of wuḍūʾ.

1 *Mustadrak al Wasāʾil*, Vol. 1, P. 42
2 Paraphrased from *Al-Kāfī*, Vol. 3, P. 71

Prerequisites for Wuḍūʾ

- All wuḍūʾ body parts must be ṭāhir (free from any najāsah).
- Water must be muṭlaq (pure), mubāh (taken with permission), and enough for wuḍūʾ.
- If using a container, it must be mubāh and not made of gold and silver.
- One must remove all barriers, like nail polish, paint, glue, and rings.
- One must have tartīb (correct order).
- One must have muwālāt (perform the wuḍūʾ without interruptions).
- There must be enough time available to perform wuḍūʾ and complete the prayer before it is qaḍāʾ.
- Water must not be harmful to one's health.
- Wuḍūʾ must be performed by oneself.

Method

Wuḍūʾ is divided into two types of actions: **mustaḥab** (recommended) and **wājib** (required) actions.

NIYYAH

Before performing wuḍūʾ and throughout the process, one must have the intention that he or she is performing wuḍūʾ to become closer to Allah.

Upon looking at the water, it is recommended to say:

بِسْمِ اللهِ وَبِاللهِ اَلْحَمْدُ لِلهِ الَّذِى جَعَلَ الْمَاءَ طَهُورًا وَلَمْ يَجْعَلْهُ نَجِسًا

Bismillāhi wa billāh. Alḥamdulillāhil-ladhī jaʿalal-māʾa ṭahīrā wa lam yajʿalhu najisā

With the name of Allah and with the help of Allah! All praise is for Allah, who made water purifying and not impure.

Mustaḥab Actions

1. WASHING THE HANDS

While washing the hands, one should say:

اَللّٰهُمَّ اجْعَلْنِي مِنَ التَّوَّابِينَ وَاجْعَلْنِي مِنَ الْمُتَطَهِّرِينَ

Allāhummaj-ʿalnī minat-tawwābīna waj-ʿalnī minal-mutaṭahhirīn

O Allah! Include me amongst those who repent and purify themselves!

2. GARGLING

While rinsing the mouth one should say:

اَللّٰهُمَّ لَقِّنِي حُجَّتِي يَوْمَ اَلْقَاكَ وَاَطْلِقْ لِسَانِي بِذِكْرَاكَ

Allāhumma laqqinī ḥujjatī yawmal-qāka wa aṭliq lisānī bidhikrāk

O Allah! Dictate to me the principles of faith on the day I meet You, and make my tongue fluent with Your remembrance.

3. TAKING WATER INTO THE NOSTRILS

While washing the nose one should say:

اَللّٰهُمَّ لَا تُحَرِّمْ عَلَيَّ رِيحَ الْجَنَّةِ وَاجْعَلْنِي مِمَّنْ يَشَمُّ رِيحَهَا وَرَوْحَهَا وَطِيبَهَا

Allāhumma lā tuḥarrim ʿalaya rīḥal-jannati waj-ʿalnī min-man yashammu rīḥaha wa rawḥaha wa ṭībahā

O Allah! Do not deprive me of the fragrance of Heaven, and include me amongst those who smell its fragrance and perfume.

Wājib Actions

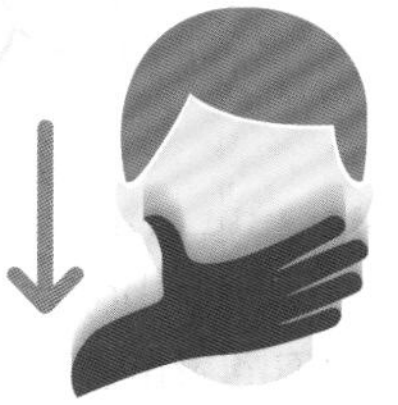

2x

4. WASHING THE FACE

- Wash the face, downwards, from above the hairline to the chin.
- The entire width between the tip of the thumb and middle finger must be wiped, including closed eyelids, eyelashes, and eye corners. To ensure the entire span has been washed, it is wājib to wash extra, both in width and length.
- Washing the face once is wājib. Washing it twice is mustaḥab. **However, washing it more than two times makes your wuḍūʾ bāṭil.***

While washing the face, one should say:

اَللّٰهُمَّ بَيِّضْ وَجْهِيْ يَوْمَ تَسْوَدُّ الْوُجُوْهُ وَلَا تُسَوِّدْ وَجْهِيْ يَوْمَ تَبْيَضُّ الْوُجُوْهُ

Allāhumma bayyiḍ wajhī yawma taswaddul-wujuhu wa lā tusawwid wajhī yawma tabyaḍḍul-wujuh
O Allah! Make my face bright on the day when the faces will turn dark! And do not darken my face on the day when the faces are bright!

*Typically, most marājiʿ say that once water has reached the entire face, it is considered as one wash. However, other marājiʿ say that the completion of a wash is based on your intention and when you decide a wash is complete. Please refer to your own marjaʿ for details.

5. WASHING THE ARMS

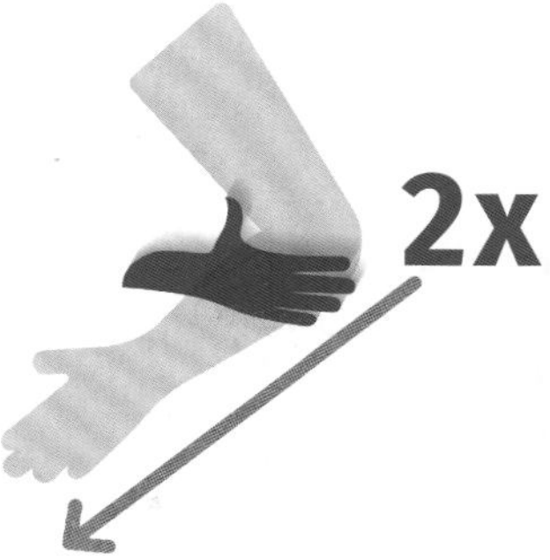

- Wash the entire arm (back and front) from above the elbow to the ends of the fingertips. The arm must be washed in a downward motion. To ensure the entire arm has been washed, it is wājib to wash a little extra (above the elbow).
- It is mustaḥab for men to start from the outer arm and for women to start from the inner arm.
- Washing the arms once is wājib. Washing them twice is mustaḥab. **However, washing them more than two times makes your wuḍūʾ bāṭil.**

While pouring water over the right arm, one should say:

اَللّٰهُمَّ اَعْطِنِیْ كِتَابِیْ بِیَمِیْنِیْ وَالْخُلْدَ فِی الْجِنَانِ بِیَسَارِیْ وَحَاسِبْنِیْ حِسَابًا یَسِیْرًا

Allāhumma āʿṭinī kitābī bi yamini wal-khulda fil-jināni biyasārī wa ḥāsibnī ḥisābān yasīrā

O Allah! Give my book of deeds in my right hand, and a permanent stay in Paradise on my left, and make my accounting easy.

While pouring water over the left arm, one should say:

اَللّٰهُمَّ لَا تُعْطِنِیْ كِتَابِیْ بِشِمَالِیْ وَلَا مِنْ وَرَاءِ ظَهْرِیْ وَلَا تَجْعَلْهَا مَغْلُوْلَةً اِلٰی عُنُقِیْ وَاَعُوْذُ بِكَ مِنْ مُقَطَّعَاتِ النِّیْرَانِ

Allāhumma la tuʿṭinī kitābī bishimālī wa lā min warāʾi ẓahrī wa lā tajʿalhā maghlūlatan ilā ʿunqī wa aʿudhu bika min muqaṭṭaʿātin-nayrān

O Allah! Do not give my book of deeds in my left hand, nor from behind my back, nor chain it to my neck. I seek refuge in You from the Hellfire.

6. MASḤ (WIPING) OF THE HEAD

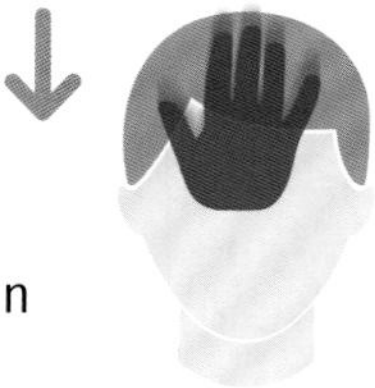

1x

- Use your right hand to wipe the roots of your hair at the top of your head. The wiping motion should begin towards the back of the head and glide to the front, without going past the hairline.
- No additional water should be taken for performing masḥ. Therefore, ensure that you turn off the tap before you finish wiping your arms so that you do not touch the wet tap before doing your masḥ. Alternatively, you may turn off the tap with the back of your hand or another part of your body that will not be coming into contact with your head during masḥ. The goal is to avoid re-wetting the palms of your hands for Steps 6 and 7.
- Your head must be dry before you wipe it.
- Only your hand should move relative to your head while wiping. In other words, keep your head still while your hand moves across it.
- Is it mustaḥab to wipe with the width of three fingers and length of one finger.

While performing the wiping of the head, one should say:

اَللّٰهُمَّ غَشِّنِيْ رَحْمَتَكَ وَبَرَكَاتِكَ

Allāhumma ghashshinī bi raḥmatika wa barakātik
O Allah! Cover me with Your mercy and blessings!

7. MASḤ (WIPING) OF THE FEET

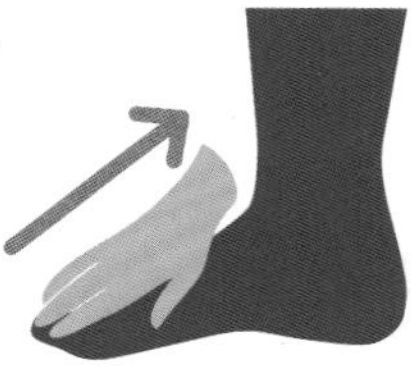

1x

- Use your right hand to wipe your right foot from the tip of the toes to the ankle. Then, wipe your left foot with your left hand in the same manner.
- No additional water should be taken.
- Your feet must be dry before you wipe them.
- Your feet should not move while you are wiping.

While performing the wiping of the feet, one should say:

اَللّٰهُمَّ ثَبِّتْنِيْ عَلَى الصِّرَاطِ يَوْمَ تَزِلُّ الْاَقْدَامُ وَاجْعَلْ سَعْيِيْ فِيْمَا يُرْضِيْكَ عَنِّيْ يَا ذَاالْجَلَالِ وَالْاِكْرَامِ

Allāhumma thabbitnī ʿalaṣ-ṣirāṭi yawma tazillul-aqdām wajʿal saʿyī fīmā yurdīkaʿannī yā dhal jalāli wal-ikrām

O Allah! Keep me firm on the bridge (to Paradise) on the day when the feet will slip, and help me in my efforts to do things that will please You, O the Lord of glory and might!

8. UPON COMPLETION, IT IS RECOMMENDED TO SAY:

اَللّٰهُمَّ اِنِّى اَسْئَلُكَ تَمَامَ الْوُضُوْءِ وَتَمَامَ ا لصَّلَاةِ وَتَمَامَ رِضْوَانِكَ وَالْجَنَّةَ

Allāhumma innī asʾaluka tamāmal-wuḍūʾi wa tamāmaṣ-ṣalāti wa tamāma riḍwānika wal-jannah

O Allah! Surely, I ask you to perfect my wuḍūʾ and ṣalāh and [allow me] attainment of Your pleasure and Heaven!

Mubṭilāt (Nullifiers) of Wuḍūʾ

There are four actions that nullify one's wuḍūʾ:

1. Passing urine or stool
2. Passing gas from the rear
3. Sleeping
4. Falling unconscious

If one has a doubt regarding whether or not they still have their wuḍūʾ, they must abide by the following principle: Certainty > Doubt. For example, if you are *certain* that you performed wuḍūʾ in the morning, but are not sure whether you performed any action since then that would nullify your wuḍūʾ, your certainty is stronger; thus, your wuḍūʾ is valid.

However, if you doubt whether or not you performed wuḍūʾ in the first place, then your doubt is stronger. As such, you must perform wuḍūʾ before offering ṣalāh.

Components of Ṣalāh

There are 11 components in the ṣalāh, which are divided into *rukn* and *ghayr rukn* categories. All are *wājib* (required) components of prayer.

- **RUKN:** *Rukn* means "a pillar" of the prayer. If you miss this during your ṣalāh or add it, intentionally or unintentionally, it will invalidate the prayer. There are five actions in the *rukn* category.

- **GHAYR RUKN:** *Ghayr* means "not." Thus, *ghayr rukn* means "not a pillar." Omitting it/incorrectly adding it intentionally will invalidate the ṣalāh. However, the ṣalāh will be fine if these actions are unintentionally added or omitted. Ṣalāh has six *ghayr rukn* components.

The chart on the opposite page outlines the mandatory components of ṣalāh, and which category each action belongs to.

As you perform the steps of ṣalāh,
remember to maintain its **order** and **continuity**:

- ***Tartīb*** means maintaining the order of actions performed in ṣalāh. Intentionally performing the actions out of order will invalidate the ṣalāh. For example, reading a different sūrah before reciting Sūrah al-Fātiḥah or going into sajdah before rukūʿ will disrupt the order of the ṣalāh, and you will need to redo that prayer.

- ***Muwālāt*** is the continuity/flow of the actions of ṣalāh, which should be performed one after another without gaps in time. This continuity preserves the rhythm of the ṣalāh.

COMPONENT	DEFINITION	RUKN	GHAYR RUKN
Niyyah (Intention)	The first obligatory act of ṣalāh. This can be said/ thought in your own language.	●	
Takbīrat al-Iḥrām	Saying “Allāhu Akbar” to begin ṣalāh. This phrase means “Allah is the Greatest.”	●	
Qiyām	The period of standing after saying the Takbīrat ul-Iḥrām, which ends right before going into rukūʿ.	●	
Qirāʾah	Qirāʾah is the recitation of Sūrah al-Fātiḥah and another small sūrah in the first two rakaʿāt.		●
Dhikr	Dhikr is any rhythmic repetition of words in praise of Allah (swt).		●
Rukūʿ	Bowing while placing hands on your knees (for men) or thighs (for women).	●	
Sajdah	Two *sajdahs* count as one *rukn*. A sajdah is a kind of prostration in which we bring seven parts of our body, most importantly the forehead, to the ground.	●	
Tashahhud	Testimony of the faith in which we bear witness to the oneness of Allah (swt) and the apostleship of His Prophet (ṣ). It is recited at the end of the **second** and **last** rakaʿāt of the prayers.		●
Salām	Salutation recited at the very end of the ṣalāh. Through salām, one exits from the state of ṣalāh.		●
Tartīb	The order of ṣalāh. One can not change the order any of the actions of ṣalāh are performed in.		●
Muwālāt	Keeping the continuity of recitation within ṣalāh without breaks.		●

The Steps of Ṣalāh

1. Niyyah (INTENTION)

"Allah will not call you to account for thoughtlessness in your oaths, but for the intention in your hearts; and He is the All-Forgiving, All-Forebearing." (2:225)

In Islam, the ***niyyah***, or intention, made before an action holds a significant role in its acceptance. A small act performed with a pure intention for the sake of Allah (swt) can be accepted and given great value. On the other hand, an action performed with great effort that isn't done with a desire for nearness to Allah (swt) or is performed without any intention can go to waste. Thus, intention is a pillar of ṣalāh as well. The niyyah starts in the heart and can be simply thought of (it does not need to be said aloud). However, if one wants to say it out-loud, it can be said in any language. While making the intention, keep in mind:

- **What action is being performed?**
  Ex: helping someone, performing ṣalāh, keeping fast, etc.
- **Why are you performing the action?**
  Ex: *fī sabīlillāh* (in the way of Allah), *qurbatan ilallāh* (for seeking nearness to Allah), etc.

Example: "I am performing a two rakaʿāt wājib Fajr ṣalāh, qurbatan ilallāh."

2. Takbīrat ul-Iḥrām

"In houses Allah has allowed to be raised and wherein His Name is celebrated; He is glorified therein, morning and evening." (24:36)

After making your intention, you are ready to begin your ṣalāh. The ṣalāh will initiate with the first takbīr. ***Takbīr*** is the Arabic phrase "Allāhu Akbar," which means "Allah is the Greatest." Saying this first takbīr in Arabic is *wājib* (required) and a rukn. It must be spoken in at least a whisper, which you yourself can hear.

1x As you begin to recite the **"Allāhu Akbar,"** it is recommended to raise both hands, with palms facing outward, towards your ears. Your hands should reach your ears by the time the recitation ends.

This first takbīr is called "Takbīrat ul-Iḥrām" because after saying this phrase, certain things become *ḥarām* (forbidden) for the person praying (such as eating, talking, drinking, etc.). During ṣalāh, only the first Takbīrat ul-Iḥrām is wājib. The remaining takbīrs performed for different actions such as bowing, siting, standing upright, etc. are simply *mustaḥab* (recommended).

3. Qiyām

"And [mention, O Muḥammad], when We designated for Abraham the site of the House, [saying], 'Do not associate anything with Me and purify My House for those who circumambulate it and those who stand [in prayer], bow, and prostrate.'" (22:26)

Qiyām is the period of standing after saying the Takbīrat ul-Iḥrām, which ends right before going into your first rukūʿ. In the state of qiyām, one is in the presence of Allah (swt). Consequently, the person praying should stand motionless and attentive during qiyām. Try your best to eliminate worldly thoughts from your mind while in this state, and seek the Almighty's help in doing so.

*NOTE: Even in situations involving praying while sitting (on a plane, or due to physical injury, for example), if you are physically able, you must stand while reciting the Takbīrat ul-Iḥrām, pause for a second, and then sit down to continue the rest of your prayer.

4. Qirā’ah

“Glorify, then, [O Prophet] the name of your Great Lord.” *(56:74)*

Qirāʾah is the recitation of sūrahs in the first two rakaʿāt of ṣalāh. While standing in the **first and second rakaʿāt**, it is required to recite **Sūrah al-Fātiḥah and another small sūrah**. When reciting:

- Try your best to pronounce the sūrahs with correct Arabic pronunciation.
- Read in a peaceful manner and do not rush.
- Make proper stops at the end of every āyah.
- Recite in a whisper during Ẓuhr and ʿAṣr prayers.
  (this is wājib for both men and women).
- Recite aloud during Fajr, Maghrib, and ʿIshāʾ prayers.
  (this is wājib for men only).

5. Dhikr

"O you who have faith! Remember Allah with frequent remembrance." (33:41)

Dhikr is the recitation of anything that reminds you of Allah (swt) and usually involves a repetition of words in praise of Him. The following dhikrs are wājib in ṣalāh and must be spoken in at least a whisper:

- Dhikr of rukūʿ
- Dhikr of sajdah
- Dhikr while standing in 3rd and 4th rakaʿāt

Although there is no mandatory dhikr for the different parts of ṣalāh, the most recommended ones have been passed down to us through the Prophet (ṣ) and Imāms (ʿa). The following sections will outline the specific dhikr that accompanies each action.

While standing during the **third and fourth rakaʿāt,** one can recite **Sūrah al-Fātiḥah once***, or it is highly recommended to recite a dhikr called ***Tasbīḥāt al-Arbaʿah:***

3x سُبْحَانَ اللهِ وَ الْحَمْدُ لِلّٰهِ وَ لَا اِلٰهَ إِلَّا اللهُ وَ اللهُ أَكْبَرُ

Subḥānallāhi, walḥamdulillāhi, wa lā ilāha illallāhu, wallāhu akbar
Glory be to Allah; all praise is for Allah; there is no god except Allah; and Allah is the Greatest

This dhikr should be recited three times out of precaution (although some marājiʿ say one time is sufficient. Please refer to your marjaʿ for details). It is wājib to recite the dhikr of the third and fourth rakaʿāt in a whisper.

*NOTE: Unlike the first two rakaʿāt, there is no second sūrah to be recited in the third and fourth rakaʿāt.

6. Rukūʿ

"And maintain the prayer, and give zakāt, and bow along with those who bow [in prayer]." (2:43)

The literal meaning of ***rukūʿ*** is "bowing down." It is one of the essential pillars of prayer. Performing it inadequately, intentionally or unintentionally, can invalidate the prayers. In our daily prayers, one rukūʿ is performed per rakʿah.

The Etiquette of Rukūʿ

After the completion of the dhikr while standing, one bends forward at the hips and places their hands on their knees while praising the Lord through dhikr. It is said that our Noble Prophet (ṣ) would bow so deeply and so straight that if a drop of water was poured onto his back, it would not fall to either side of him.

There are slight differences in how men and women perform rukūʿ. The recommendations are outlined below:

WOMEN

- Bend in an arch-like form
- Hands on thighs, just above knees
- Elbows kept closer to body

MEN

- Bend at a 90-degree angle
- Hands on knees
- Elbows away from body

During rukūʿ, focus your gaze on the ground between your feet and recite the following dhikr at least once, although three times is recommended:

3x 1x سُبْحَانَ رَبِّيَ الْعَظِيمِ وَ بِحَمْدِهِ

Subḥāna rabbiyal-ʿaẓīmi wa biḥamdih

Glory be to my Lord, the Supreme, and praise belongs to Him

Alternately, one may also recite the following dhikr three times:

3x سُبْحَانَ اللهِ

Subḥānallāh

Glory be to Allah

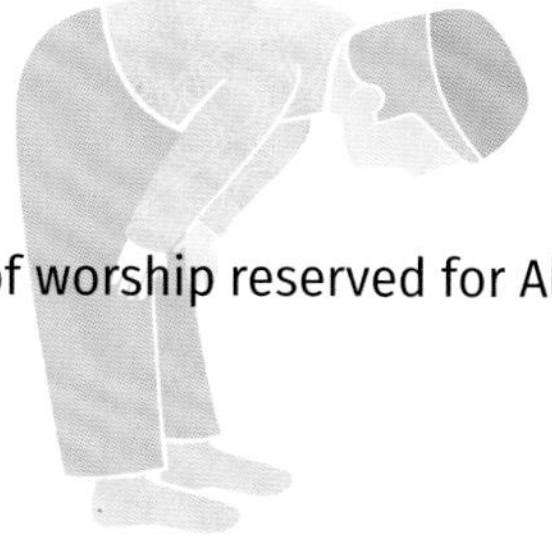

Rukūʿ and sajdah are specific positions of worship reserved for Allah (swt) alone. Their sequence during ṣalāh is important, as the actions complement one another.

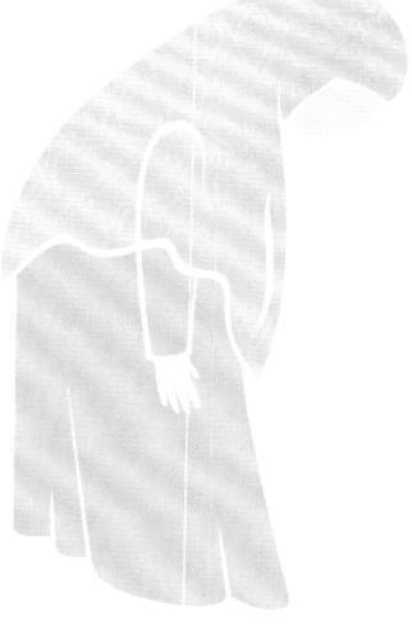

Imām aṣ-Ṣādiq (ʿa) has said:

"A long rukuʿ and sujud have effects on the longevity of life."

(*Wasāʾil ash-Shīʿah*, Vol. 4, P. 928)

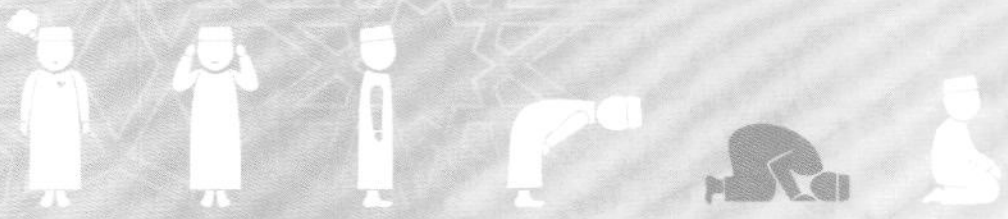

7. Sajdah

"O Mary, be obedient to your Lord, and prostrate." (3:43)

Sajdah is the action of placing one's forehead to the ground as a demonstration of humility and submission to Allah (swt). In ṣalāh, two sajdahs count as one rukn, and they are performed after the rukūʿ.

During sajdah, seven parts of the body should touch the ground. These parts are:

- The forehead
- Both palms
- Both knees
- Both big toes

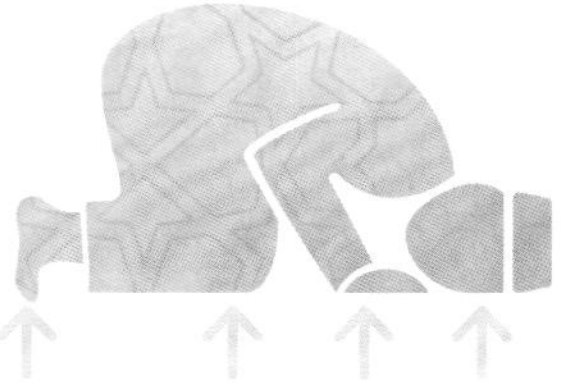

There are slight differences in how men and women perform sajdah. The recommendations are outlined below:

WOMEN

- Feet close together during sajdah
- Arms kept closer to body

MEN

- Feet apart during sajdah
- Arms away from body

The following dhikr should be recited while in sajdah:

1x سُبْحَانَ رَبِّيَ الْأَعْلَىٰ وَ بِحَمْدِهِ

Subḥāna rabbiyal-aʿlā wa biḥamdih
Glory be to my Lord, the Exalted, and praise belongs to Him

Alternately, one may also recite the following dhikr three times:

3x سُبْحَانَ اللّٰه

Subḥānallāh.
Glory be to Allah.

When sitting up between and after sajdah, it is recommended to sit with the right foot on top of the left.

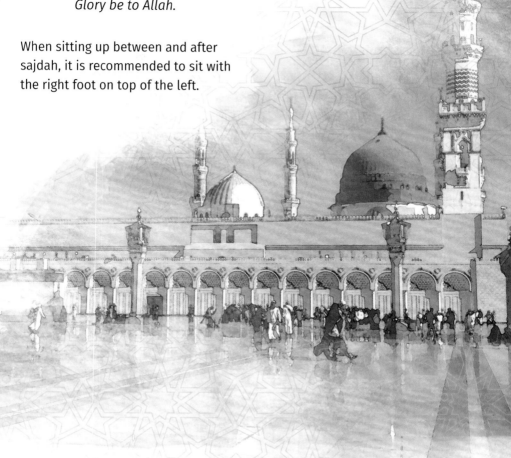

7. Sajdah (CONTINUED)

Permissible Objects for Sajdah

Sajdah must be performed on the earth or on what grows from it, with the exception of anything that is edible or wearable by humans.

Examples of what one CAN perform sajdah on: ✔	Examples of what one CANNOT perform sajdah on: ✘
• **Turbah** (soil or dirt - recommended) • **Stones** • **Wood** • **Leaves/grass/hay** (only those which are inedible for humans)	• **Precious metals/stones** such as gold, silver, rubies, etc. (can be worn) • **Clothing material** such as cotton (which comes from the earth, but can be worn) • **Fruits, vegetables, grains** (all edible by humans)

Among all the items sajdah may be performed on, prostration on the soil of Karbalāʾ (commonly known as turbah of Karbalāʾ) is the most recommended. According to tradition, performing sajdah on turbah elevates the quality of the prayers, by virtue of the sacrifice Imām Ḥusayn (ʿa) made for the sake of Allah (swt) to save Islam. Prostration on turbah reminds us of this sacrifice and symbolizes that we embrace wilāyah (the divine leadership) in reaching our Lord.

Prostration of Thanks (Shukr)

Once your ṣalāh is finished, it is recommended to perform one final sajdah as a token of thanks and obedience. In this Sajdah ash-Shukr, or "Prostration of Thanks," we thank Allah (swt) for giving us the opportunity to perform ṣalāh and remember His blessings upon us.

There are multiple duʿās and dhikr that can be recited in Sajdah ash-Shukr. The simplest of these is thanking Allah (swt) by reciting:

شُكْرًا لِلّٰهِ

Shukranlillāh

All thanks is for Allah

The Philosophy of Sajdah

When asked about the symbolism behind sajdah, Imām ʿAlī (ʿa) said, "The first sajdah symbolizes that my existence began as dust, and as I raise my head from sajdah, it signifies that I came into the world from that dust. The second sajdah signifies that I will again return to the soil, and as I raise my head from sajdah, it symbolizes that on the Day of Resurrection, I will rise up from the grave and be summoned."

Sajdah brings us closer to Allah (swt) by breaking our pride and arrogance. The person praying should perform the sajdah with sincerity and keep in mind that his/her prostrations are solely for the Creator.

8. Tashahhud

"Allah bears witness that there is no god but Him – and (so do) the angels and those who possess knowledge." *(3:18)*

Tashahhud is the testimony of our faith in which we bear witness to the oneness of Allah (swt) and the apostleship (*risālah*) of His Prophet Muḥammad (ṣ). It is recited in the **second** and **last** rakaʿāt of the prayers. It is *wājib* (obligatory) to recite it once in two-rakaʿāt prayers and twice in three or four-rakaʿāt prayers. Omitting the tashahhud intentionally during ṣalāh will invalidate the prayers (but if done unintentionally, the prayer will still be valid).

As you come up from sajdah, sit on your heels with your right foot over your left (right/left foot positioning is recommended, but not required). Place your hands on your thighs as you recite the following:

1x

أَشْهَدُ أَنْ لَا اِلٰهَ إِلَّا اللّٰهُ وَحْدَهُ لَا شَرِيْكَ لَه
وَأَشْهَدُ أَنَّ مُحَمَّدًا عَبْدُهُ وَ رَسُوْلُه

Ashhadu an-lā ilāha illallāh, waḥdahu lā sharīka lah, wa ashhadu anna Muḥammadan ʿabduhu wa rasūluh
I bear witness that there is no god except Allah, the One, with no partner to Him, and I bear witness that Muḥammad is His servant and Messenger

The tashahhud reminds us of the supremacy of our Lord — that He alone is worthy of worship and has no partner or equal. The testimony of *risālah* (attesting to the prophethood of Prophet Muḥammad) is a reminder that we accept Allah's appointed guide and we recognize Him through His divinely appointed messenger, Prophet Muḥammad (ṣ).

Note that in the calls to prayer (the *adhān* and *iqāmah*) at the beginning of ṣalāh, we testify to the oneness of Allah (swt) and the apostleship of the Prophet (ṣ). We wrap up the prayer with the same two attestations, a purposeful reminder of the foundations of our faith.

After completing the tashahhud, it is wājib to recite *ṣalawāt*, a phrase that is a symbol of our love for the the Prophet (ṣ) and his divine household (ʿa).

The ṣalawāt is recited as follows:

1x أَللَّهُمَّ صَلِّ عَلٰى مُحَمَّدٍ وَّ آلِ مُحَمَّدٍ

Allāhumma ṣalli ʿalā Muḥammad wa āli Muḥammad
O Allah, send blessings on Muḥammad and the family of Muḥammad

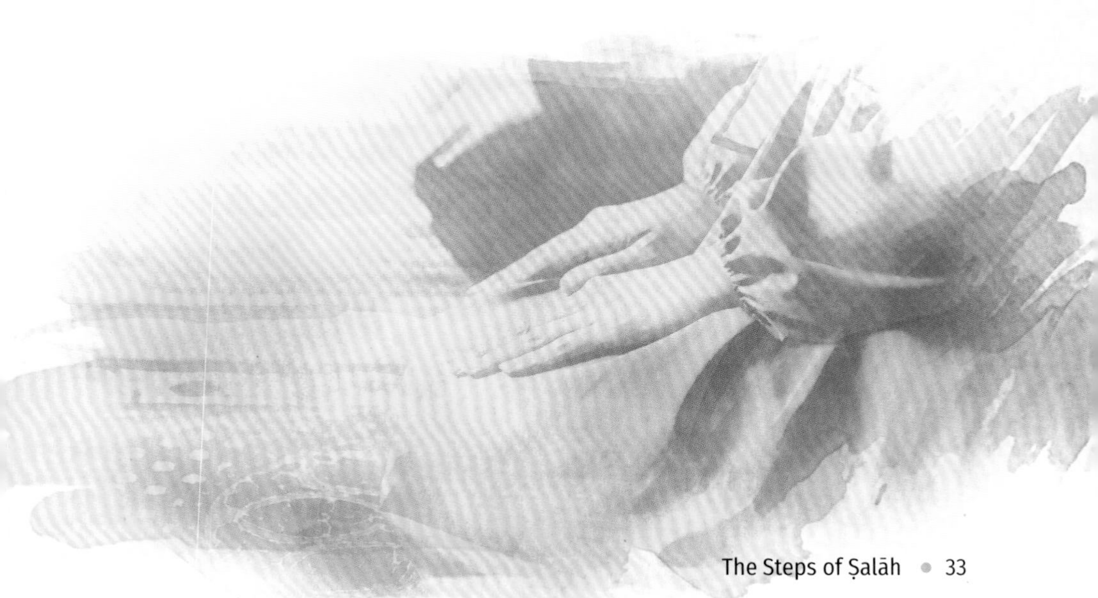

9. Salām

"Indeed, Allah and His angels send blessings upon the Prophet. O you who believe, send blessings upon him and greet him with peace."
(33:56)

Salām, or salutation, is the last part of ṣalāh. Through salām, one exits from the state of ṣalāh. This particular salām contains three phrases: the first we send upon the Prophet of Allah (ṣ), the second upon all the other Prophets and the infallible Imāms, and lastly upon all the believers and the angels.

First Phrase (highly recommended):

اَلسَّلَامُ عَلَيْكَ اَيُّهَا النَّبِيُّ وَ رَحْمَةُ اللهِ وَ بَرَكَاتُه 1x

As-salāmu ʿalayka ayyuhan-nabiyyu wa raḥmatul-lāhi wa barakātuh

Peace be upon you, O Prophet, and Allah's mercy and His blessing [be upon you]

Second Phrase (obligatory):

اَلسَّلَامُ عَلَيْنَا وَ عَلٰى عِبَادِ اللهِ الصَّالِحِيْنَ 1x

As-salāmu ʿalaynā wa ʿalā ʿibādil-lāhiṣ-ṣāliḥīn

Peace be upon us and upon the righteous servants of Allah

Third Phrase (obligatory):

اَلسَّلَامُ عَلَيْكُمْ وَ رَحْمَةُ اللهِ وَ بَرَكَاتُه 1x

As-salāmu ʿalaykum wa raḥmatul-lāhi wa barakātuh

Peace be upon you all, and Allah's mercy and blessings [be upon you]

Two Rakaʿāt Ṣalāh at a Glance

FIRST RAKAʿĀT

POSITION	WHAT TO RECITE
	Niyyah & **Takbīrat ul-Iḥrām**
	**Sūrah al-Fātiḥah & 2nd Sūrah**
	**Dhikr of Rukūʿ**
	*Samiʿal-lāhu liman ḥamidah*
	**Dhikr of Sajdah**
	*Astaghfirul-lāha rabbī wa atūbū ilayh*
	**Dhikr of Sajdah**
	Sit and pause for a second

SECOND RAKAʿĀT

POSITION	WHAT TO RECITE
	Stand up while saying: ***Biḥawlil-lāhi wa quwwatihi aqumu wa aqʿud***
	**Sūrah al-Fātiḥah & 2nd Sūrah**
	**Dhikr of Rukūʿ**
	*Samiʿal-lāhu liman ḥamidah*
	**Dhikr of Sajdah**
	*Astaghfirul-lāha rabbī wa atūbū ilayh*
	**Dhikr of Sajdah**
	**Tashahhud & Salām**

Three Rakaʿāt Ṣalāh Step by Step

Let's learn how to recite a three rakaʿāt ṣalāh with minimum obligatory recitation (wājib dhikr). To make this a four rakaʿāt ṣalāh, omit the tashahhud and salām from the third rakʿah, and repeat the steps of the third rakʿah in the fourth rakʿah, ending with tashahhud and salām.

Niyyah

I am performing a three rakaʿāt wājib Maghrib ṣalāh, qurbatan ilallāh.

Takbīrat al-Iḥrām

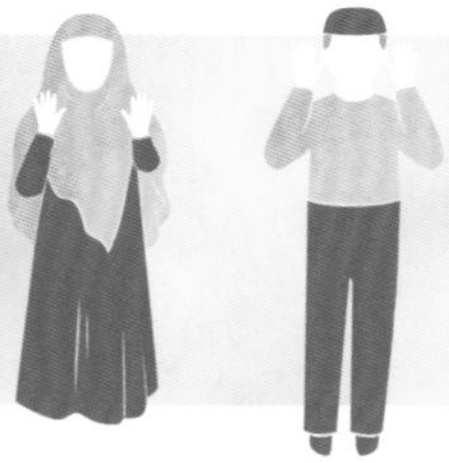

Allāhu Akbar

QIRA'AT: Sūrah al-Fātiḥah

- *Bismillāhir Raḥmānir Raḥīm*
- *Alḥamdulillāhi rabbil-ʿālamīn*
- *Ar-raḥmānir-raḥīm*
- *Māliki yawmid-dīn*
- *Iyyāka naʿbudū wa iyyāka nastaʿīn*
- *Ihdinaṣ-ṣirātal mustaqīm*
- *Ṣirātal-ladhīna anʿamta ʿalayhim*
- *Ghayril-maghḍūbī ʿalayhim wa laḍ-ḍāllīn*

Sūrah al-Ikhlāṣ*

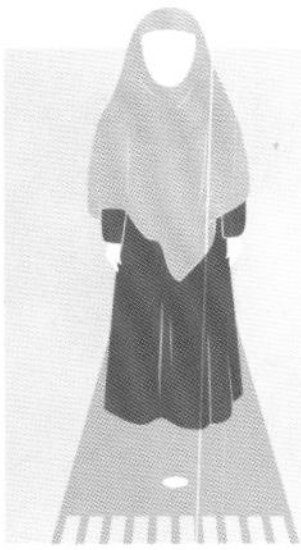

- *Bismillāhir Raḥmānir Raḥīm*
- *Qul huwallāhu aḥad*
- *Allāhuṣ-ṣamad*
- *Lam yalid wa lam yūlad*
- *Wa lam ya kun-lahu kufuwan aḥad*

Rukūʿ

Subḥāna rabbiyal-ʿaẓīmi wa biḥamdih
OR
Subḥānallāh, subḥānallāh, subḥānallāh

Qiyām

Samiʿal-lāhu liman ḥamidah

1st Sajdah

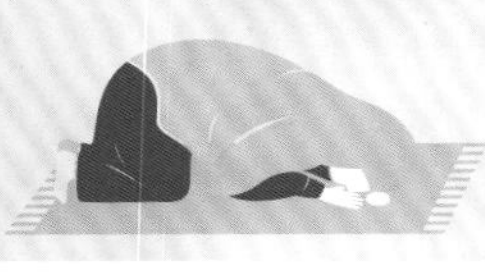

Subḥāna rabbiyal-aʿlā wa biḥamdih
OR
Subḥānallāh, subḥānallāh, subḥānallāh

Julūs (sitting)

Astaghfirul-lāha rabbī wa atūbu ilayh

2nd Sajdah

Subḥāna rabbiyal-aʿlā wa biḥamdih
OR
Subḥānallāh, subḥānallāh, subḥānallāh

*Can read any other complete sūrah

THREE RAKAʿĀT ṢALĀH: STEP BY STEP *continued*

Julūs (sitting)

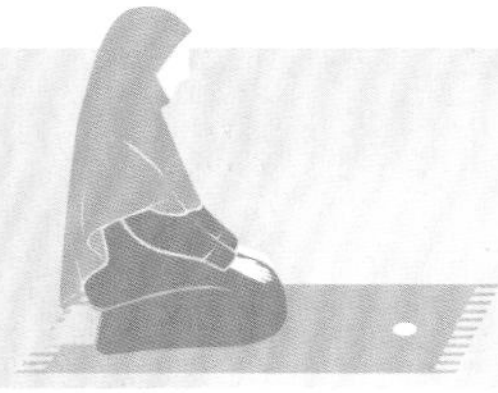

Sit and pause for a second. Then, stand up while saying:
Biḥawlil-lāhi wa quwwatihi aqumu wa aqʿud

QIRA'AT: Sūrah al-Fātiḥah

- *Bismillāhir Raḥmānir Raḥīm*
- *Alḥamdulillāhi rabbil-ʿālamīn*
- *Ar-raḥmānir-raḥīm*
- *Māliki yawmid-dīn*
- *Iyyāka naʿbudū wa iyyāka nastaʿīn*
- *Ihdinaṣ-ṣirātal mustaqīm*
- *Ṣirātal-ladhīna anʿamta ʿalayhim*
- *Ghayril-maghḍūbī ʿalayhim wa laḍ-ḍāllīn*

Sūrah al-Ikhlāṣ*

- *Bismillāhir Raḥmānir Raḥīm*
- *Qul huwallāhu aḥad*
- *Allāhuṣ-ṣamad*
- *Lam yalid wa lam yūlad*
- *Wa lam ya kun-lahu kufuwan aḥad*

Rukūʿ

Subḥāna rabbiyal-ʿaẓīmi wa biḥamdih
OR
Subḥānallāh, subḥānallāh, subḥānallāh

*Can read any other complete sūrah

Qiyām

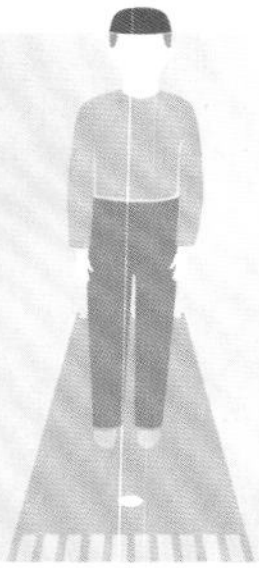

Sami'al-lāhu liman ḥamidah

Sajdah

Subḥāna rabbiyal-a'lā wa biḥamdih
OR
Subḥānallāh, subḥānallāh, subḥānallāh

Julūs (sitting)

Astaghfirul-lāha rabbī wa atūbu ilayh

Sajdah

Subḥāna rabbiyal-a'lā wa biḥamdih
OR
Subḥānallāh, subḥānallāh, subḥānallāh

Tashahhud

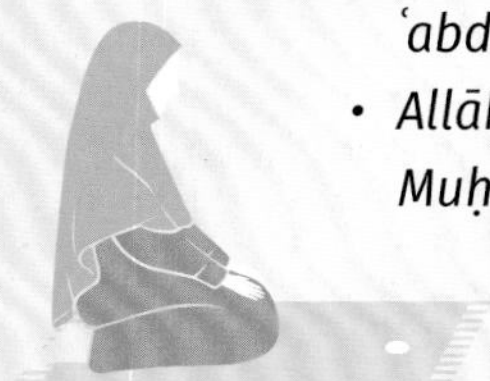

- *Ashhadu an-lā ilāha illallāhu, waḥdahu lā sharīka lah, wa ashhadu anna Muḥammadan 'abduhu wa rasūluh*
- *Allāhumma ṣalli 'alā Muḥammad wa āli Muḥammad*

Then, stand up while saying:

Biḥawlil-lāhi wa quwwatihi aqumu wa aq'ud

THREE RAKAʿĀT ṢALĀH: STEP BY STEP *continued*

Tasbīḥāt al-Arbaʿāh*

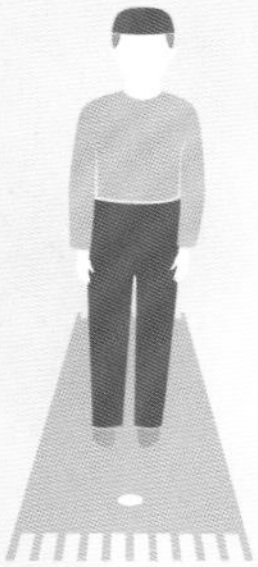

- *Subḥānallāhi, walḥamdulillāhi, wa lā ilāha illallāhu, wallāhu akbar*
- *Subḥānallāhi, walḥamdulillāhi, wa lā ilāha illallāhu, wallāhu akbar*
- *Subḥānallāhi, walḥamdulillāhi, wa lā ilāha illallāhu, wallāhu akbar*

Rukūʿ

Subḥāna rabbiyal-ʿaẓīmi wa biḥamdih
OR
Subḥānallāh, subḥānallāh, subḥānallāh

Qiyām

Samiʿal-lāhu liman ḥamidah

Sajdah

Subḥāna rabbiyal-aʿlā wa biḥamdih
OR
Subḥānallāh, subḥānallāh, subḥānallāh

*Can read any other complete sūrah

Julūs (sitting)

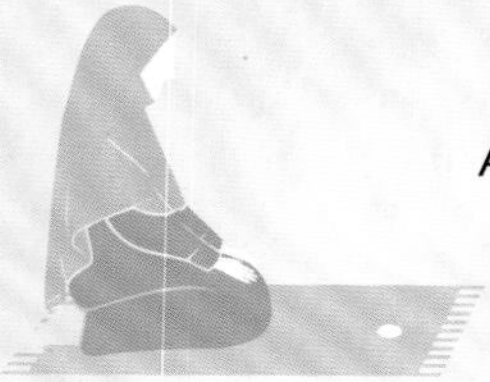

Astaghfirul-lāha rabbī wa atūbu ilayh

Sajdah

Subḥāna rabbiyal-aʿlā wa biḥamdih
OR
Subḥānallāh, subḥānallāh, subḥānallāh

Tashahhud

- *Ashhadu an-lā ilāha illallāhu, waḥdahu lā sharīka lah, wa ashhadu anna Muḥammadan ʿabduhu wa rasūluh*
- *Allāhumma ṣalli ʿalā Muḥammad wa āli Muḥammad*

Salām

- *As-salāmu ʿalayka ayyuhan-nabiyyu wa raḥmatul-lāhi wa barakātuh*
- *As-salāmu ʿalaynā wa ʿalā ʿibādil-lāhiṣ-ṣāliḥīn*
- *As-salāmu ʿalaykum wa raḥmatul-lāhi wa barakātuh*

Sūrah al-Fātiḥah

بِسْمِ اللَّـهِ الرَّحْمَٰنِ الرَّحِيمِ ﴿١﴾

Bismillāhir Raḥmānir Raḥīm

I begin, dedicate my action, and seek help with the name of Allah, the Most Kind (general mercy), the Most Merciful (mercy for the believers).

اَلْحَمْدُ لِلَّـهِ رَبِّ الْعَالَمِينَ ﴿٢﴾

Alḥamdulillāhi rabbil-ʿālamīn

All praise is for Allah, Nurturer of the worlds.

اَلرَّحْمَٰنِ الرَّحِيمِ ﴿٣﴾

Ar-raḥmānir-raḥīm

The Most Kind (general mercy), the Most Merciful (mercy for the believers).

مَالِكِ يَوْمِ الدِّيْنِ ﴿٤﴾

Māliki yawmid-dīn

He is the Owner of the Day of Judgment.

إِيَّاكَ نَعْبُدُ وَإِيَّاكَ نَسْتَعِيْنُ ﴿٥﴾

Iyyāka naʿbudu wa iyyāka nastaʿīn

(O Allah), only You we worship, and only You we seek help from.

اِهْدِنَا الصِّرَاطَ الْمُسْتَقِيْمَ ﴿٦﴾

Ihdinaṣ-ṣirāṭ al-mustaqīm

Keep us on the straight path (and keep guiding us).

صِرَاطَ الَّذِيْنَ أَنْعَمْتَ عَلَيْهِمْ

Ṣirāṭal-ladhīna anʿamta ʿalayhim

The path of those whom You have given Your blessings (like the Prophets, Imams and Shuhadah),

---

غَيْرِ الْمَغْضُوْبِ عَلَيْهِمْ وَلَا الضَّآ لِّيْنَ ﴿٧﴾

Ghayril-maghḍūbi ʿalayhim wa laḍ-ḍāllīn

not those who are on the wrong path and have gone astray.

Sūrah al-Ikhlāṣ

بِسْمِ اللَّـهِ الرَّحْمَٰنِ الرَّحِيمِ

Bismillāhir Raḥmānir Raḥīm

I begin, dedicate my action, and seek help with the name of Allah, the Most Kind (general mercy), the Most Merciful (mercy for the believers).

قُلْ هُوَ اللَّـهُ أَحَدٌ ﴿١﴾

Qul huwal-lāhu aḥad

Say: He is Allah, the One.

اَللَّـهُ الصَّمَدُ ﴿٢﴾

Allāhuṣ-ṣamad

Allah is Absolute and Perfect (therefore He is needless).

لَمْ يَلِدْ وَلَمْ يُولَدْ ﴿٣﴾

Lam yalid wa lam yūlad

He does not have parents (He does not need a creator) and He does not give birth (He is a Unique Creator).

وَلَمْ يَكُن لَّهُ كُفُوًا أَحَدٌ ﴿٤﴾

Wa lam ya kun-lahu kufuwan aḥad

And there is no one comparable to Him.

Mustaḥabbāt of Ṣalāh

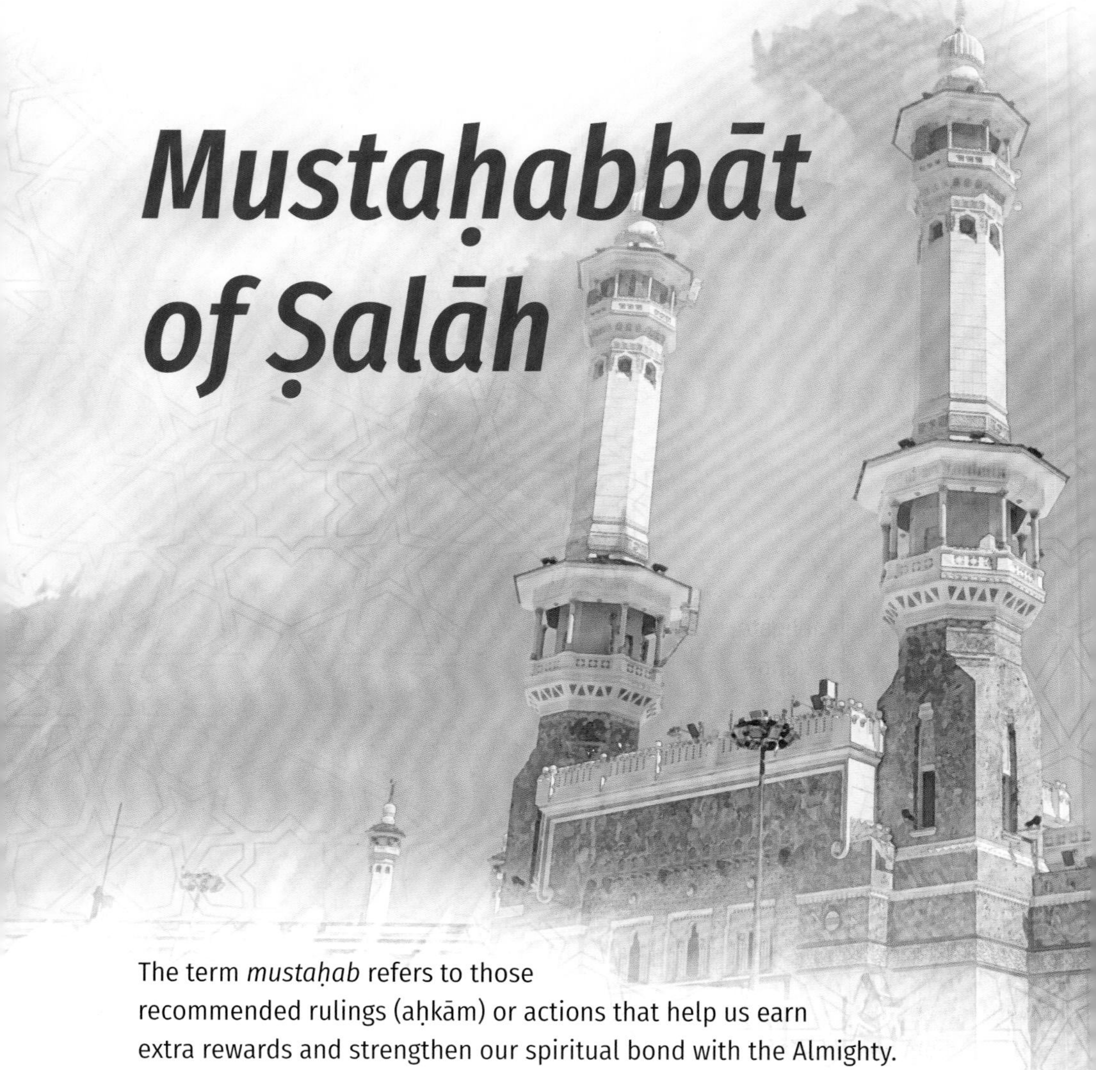

The term *mustaḥab* refers to those recommended rulings (aḥkām) or actions that help us earn extra rewards and strengthen our spiritual bond with the Almighty.

This section will focus on covering some of the mustaḥab actions of ṣalāh. It is important to only slowly introduce these practices as we become better in improving our ṣalāh. One should adopt a few of these mustaḥab actions at a time and get accustomed to them first before introducing new ones.

Following the above method will help us maintain our attention and focus during ṣalāh, while helping us adhere to the mustaḥab actions for a long time.

1. Adhān & Iqāmah

"In houses Allah has allowed to be raised and wherein His Name is celebrated; He is glorified therein, morning and evening." (24:36)

The recitation of the adhān and iqāmah is mustaḥab for both men and women before the daily obligatory prayers. The word adhān means "announcement" and is commonly defined as "the call to prayer." This is an invitation to all Muslims toward ṣalāh. Iqāmah is derived from the word "qiyām," which means "establishing [the prayers]." The iqāmah is the second call to ṣalāh, which is recited immediately before the prayers begin.

Calling the adhān and iqāmah before the ṣalāh prepares us to stand in front of the Almighty before the commencement of our worship.

The adhān and iqāmah help us establish a close proximity with our Creator while enabling us to disconnect from the worldly affairs and focusing our thoughts on our ṣalāh.

Imām aṣ-Ṣādiq (ʿa) has said:

"One who offers his prayers with adhān and iqāmah, two rows of angels pray behind him, while one who only prays with iqāmah and without adhān, only one row of angels prays behind him."

The Imām was asked, "And how long is each row?"

He replied, "At the very minimum, the distance is from the east to the west, while at the maximum, its length is the distance between the earth and the Heavens."

(*Wasāʾil ash-Shīʿah*, Vol. 4, P. 620)

Although the iqāmah is quite similar to the adhān, there are a few differences, which can be seen in the chart below.

Adhān		Iqāmah	
اَللّٰهُ اَكْبَرُ ***Allāhu Akbar*** Allah (God) is the Greatest	4x	اَللّٰهُ اَكْبَرُ ***Allāhu Akbar*** Allah (God) is the Greatest	2x
اَشْهَدُ اَنْ لَا اِلٰهَ اِلَّا اللّٰهُ ***Ashhadu an-lā ilāha illallāh*** I testify that there is no god except Allah	2x	اَشْهَدُ اَنْ لَا اِلٰهَ اِلَّا اللّٰهُ ***Ashhadu an-lā ilāha illallāh*** I testify that there is no god except Allah	2x
اَشْهَدُ اَنَّ مُحَمَّدً رَّسُوْلُ اللّٰهِ ***Ashhadu anna Muḥammadar Rasūlullāh*** I testify that Muḥammad is the messenger of Allah	2x	اَشْهَدُ اَنَّ مُحَمَّدً رَّسُوْلُ اللّٰهِ ***Ashhadu anna Muḥammadar Rasūlullāh*** I testify that Muḥammad is the messenger of Allah	2x
اَشْهَدُ اَنَّ عَلِيًّا وَّلِيُّ اللّٰهِ ***Ashhadu anna ʿAliyyan-walīyullāh*** I testify that ʿAlī is the vicegerent and close guardian of Allah	2x	اَشْهَدُ اَنَّ عَلِيًّا وَّلِيُّ اللّٰهِ ***Ashhadu anna ʿAliyyan-walīyullāh*** I testify that ʿAlī is the vicegerent and close guardian of Allah	2x
حَيَّ عَلَى الصَّلٰوةِ ***Ḥayya ʿalaṣ-ṣalāh*** Hasten to the prayer	2x	حَيَّ عَلَى الصَّلٰوةِ ***Ḥayya ʿalaṣ-ṣalāh*** Hasten to the prayer	2x
حَيَّ عَلَى الْفَلَاحِ ***Ḥayya ʿalal-falāḥ*** Hasten to success	2x	حَيَّ عَلَى الْفَلَاحِ ***Ḥayya ʿalal-falāḥ*** Hasten to success	2x
حَيَّ عَلَى خَيْرِ الْعَمَلِ ***Ḥayya ʿalā khayril-ʿamal*** Hasten to the best action	2x	حَيَّ عَلَى خَيْرِ الْعَمَلِ ***Ḥayya ʿalā khayril-ʿamal*** Hasten to the best action	2x
		قَدْ قَامَتِ الصَّلٰوةُ ***Qad qāmatiṣ-ṣalāh*** Establish the prayer!	2x
اَللّٰهُ اَكْبَرُ ***Allāhu Akbar*** Allah (God) is the Greatest	2x	اَللّٰهُ اَكْبَرُ ***Allāhu Akbar*** Allah (God) is the Greatest	2x
لَا اِلٰهَ اِلَّا اللّٰهُ ***Lā ilāha illallāh*** There is no god except Allah	2x	لَا اِلٰهَ اِلَّا اللّٰهُ ***Lā ilāha illallāh*** There is no god except Allah	1x

2. Qunūt

"And remember the name of your Lord and devote yourself to Him with [complete] devotion." (73:8)

The word ***qunūt*** can be translated as "obedience, piety, or submissiveness." According to aḥādīth, although it is one of the mustaḥab acts of ṣalāh, this is one recommended action that shouldn't be neglected. It is the part of prayer where we are given the opportunity to both ask for our desires or praise Allah. The purpose of qunūt is to bring humility in oneself, for when we raise our hands in the sense of begging from Allah, we should lower ourselves and break our pride.

PLACE OF QUNŪT:

In all the obligatory prayers, the place of qunūt is after the qirāʾah and before rukūʿ in the second rakʿah. In some occasional prayers, the place of qunūt can differ depending upon the method of that prayer. Below are some examples:

- In the Friday prayer, each rakʿah has a qunūt
- Ṣalāt al-Āyāt has five qunūts
- Eid al-Fiṭr and Eid al-Aḍḥā prayers each have nine qunūts

Imām ar-Riḍā (ʿa) has said:

"Qunūt is a highly recommended sunnah in all the daily prayers."

(*Biḥār al-Anwar*, Vol. 82, P. 197)

2. Qunūt (CONTINUED)

HOW TO PERFORM QUNŪT:

After completing the qirāʾah of the 2nd rakʿah, it is recommended to say takbīr and raise your hands in duʿā in front of your face. The hands and fingers, except the thumbs, should be kept together in this state. One should be looking towards the palms while reciting dhikr or asking Allah for fulfillment of desires. It is mustaḥab to recite the qunūt loudly, unless one is in a congregational prayer.

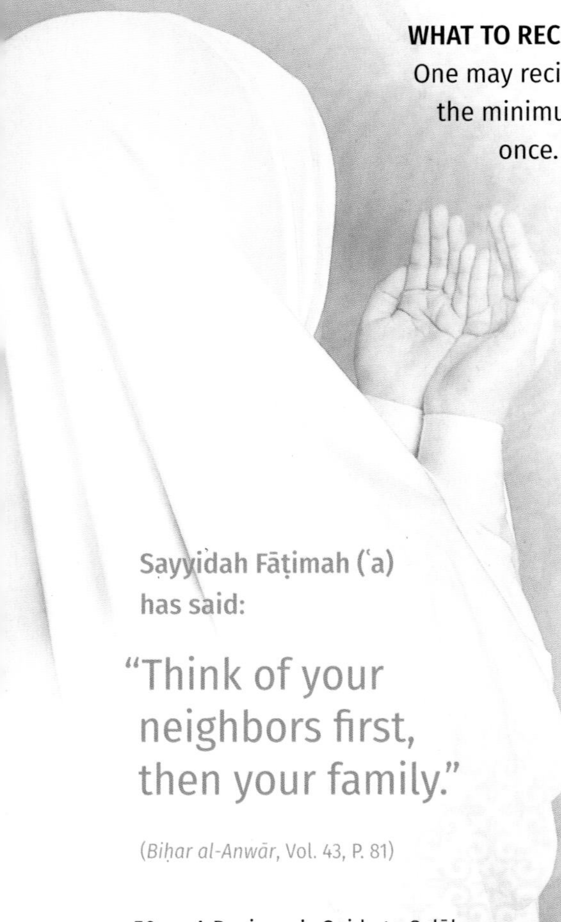

WHAT TO RECITE IN QUNŪT:

One may recite any dhikr or duʿāʾ in qunūt. At the minimum, one should say "Subḥānallāh" once. Qunūt can also be recited in one's own language; however, various supplications are provided for us to recite in qunūt. It is highly recommended to remember the Imām of our time in the state of qunūt and to recite Duʿā al-Faraj in at least one of the daily prayers. It is recommended to pray for other muʾminīn in qunūt. The recitation of salawāt should also not be neglected in this important act of worship. The salawāt has countless rewards, and reading it in the state of qunūt along with other duʿās will elevate the mustaḥab rewards of qunūt.

Sayyidah Fāṭimah (ʿa) has said:

"Think of your neighbors first, then your family."

(*Biḥar al-Anwār*, Vol. 43, P. 81)

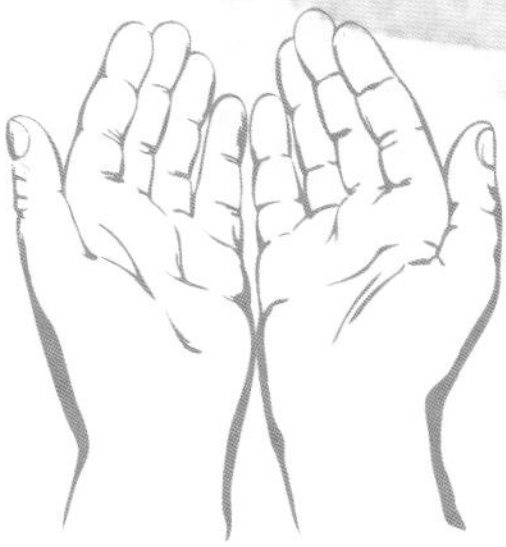

SUPPLICATIONS (DUʿĀS) FOR QUNŪT:

There are several supplications one can recite in the state of qunūt. Below are a few that are highly recommended by the Prophet (ṣ) and Ahl al-Bayt (ʿa):

رَبَّنَا آتِنَا فِى الدُّنْيَا حَسَنَةً وَّفِى الْآخِرَةِ حَسَنَةً وَّقِنَا عَذَابَ النَّارِ O

Rabbanā ātinā fid-dunyā ḥasanah wa fil ākhirati ḥasanah wa qinā ʿadhāban-nār

Our Lord, give us good in this world and good in the Hereafter, and save us from the punishment of the fire. (2:201)

رَبَّنَا اغْفِرْ لِىْ وَلِوَالِدَيَّ وَلِلْمُؤْمِنِيْنَ يَوْمَ يَقُوْمُ الْحِسَابُ O

Rabbanagh-fir lī wa liwālidayya wa lil-muʾminīna yawma yaqūmul-ḥisāb

Our Lord, forgive me, my parents, and the believers when the day of accounting is held. (14:41)

رَبِّ اجْعَلْنِىْ مُقِيْمَ الصَّلَاةِ وَمِنْ ذُرِّيَّتِىْ رَبَّنَا وَتَقَبَّلْ دُعَآءِ O

Rabbij-ʿalnī muqīmaṣ-ṣalāti wa min dhurrīyatī; Rabbanā wa taqabbal duʿāʾ

O my Lord, make me and my offspring steadfast in prayer. Our Lord, accept my supplication! (14:40)

3. Tasbīḥ az-Zahrā' ('a)

"Allah is not worshipped by anything more meritorious than the tasbīḥ of Fāṭimah az-Zahrā' ('a). Had there been any worship superior to it, most surely the Noble Prophet (ṣ) would have granted it to Sayyidah Fāṭimah ('a.)."

- Imām al-Bāqir ('a) (Wasā'il ash-Shī'ah, Vol. 4 P. 1024)

Amongst the many Mustaḥabbāt of ṣalāh, Tasbīḥ az-Zahrā' ('a) holds a special place. This simple, yet powerful, act of worship was a gift to Sayyidah Fāṭimah Zahrā' ('a) from her father, Prophet Muhammad (s). The virtues of this tasbīḥ have been recorded through various aḥādīth.

Recitation of this tasbīḥ will not only benefit the reciter's worldly affairs, but reciting this tasbīḥ while understanding its merits and out of love for Sayyidah Zahrā' ('a) will help them in the hereafter, as well.

HISTORY OF TASBĪḤ AZ-ZAHRĀ' ('A):
It has been narrated that once Sayyidah Fāṭimah ('a) requested for some assistance in completing her house chores. Imām 'Alī ('a) then directed her to seek this request from Rasūlullāh (ṣ). When Sayyidah Zahrā' presented her wish about having a maid to the Prophet (ṣ), he replied, "O Fāṭimah! I have granted you something that is superior to a maidservant and to the world and everything in it."*

He then taught her to say:

Allāhu Akbar 34x   ***Alḥamdulillāh*** 33x   ***Subḥānallāh*** 33x

*(*Āsāro Asrāreh Tasbīḥ az-Zahrā'* ('a) , P. 7)

Allāhu Akbar 34x
Alḥamdulillāh 33x
Subḥānallāh 33x

THE PLACE OF TASBĪḤ AZ-ZAHRĀʾ (ʿA) IN ṢALĀH:

Tasbīḥ az-Zahrāʾ should be recited immediately after the ṣalāh is concluded. It is recommended to remain seated in the same position in which one concludes the ṣalāh and recite this tasbīḥ.

Imām Jaʿfar aṣ-Ṣādiq (ʿa) has said :

"One who recites the tasbīḥ of Sayyidah Zahrāʾ (ʿa) after an obligatory ṣalāh, before he stretches out his legs (i.e., he recites the tasbīḥ while he is in the posture of tashahhud), then Heaven becomes obligatory upon him."

(*Falāḥ as-Sāʾil*, P. 165)

"One who recites the tasbīḥ of Sayyidah Zahrāʾ (ʿa) before even moving his feet, Allah will forgive him."

(*Tahdhīb al-Aḥkām*, Vol. 2, P. 105)

Imām al-Bāqir (ʿa) has said:

"One who recites the tasbīḥ of Sayyidah Zahrāʾ (ʿa) and then seeks forgiveness will be forgiven."

(*Wasāʾil ash-Shīʿah, Vol 4, P. 1023*)

It is highly recommended to recite this tasbīḥ on the rosary made from the soil of Karbalāʾ, as this carries numerous rewards.

It has been narrated from Imām al-Mahdī (ʿaj), "Even if one just holds the tasbīḥ made out of the soil of the grave of Imām Ḥusayn (ʿa) and does not do any dhikr, for him will be written the reward of having recited the adhkār"

(*Wasāʾil ash-Shīʿah*, Vol. 4, P. 1033)

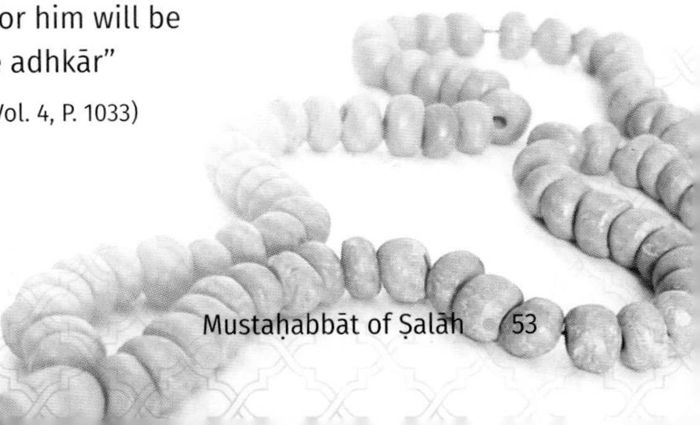

more Mustaḥabbāt of Ṣalāh

COMPONENT	RECOMMENDED ACTIONS
Takbīrat al-Iḥrām	• Saying "Allāhu Akbar" 6 times while considering it mustaḥab before making the final 7th takbīr. The 7th and final takbīr should be considered "Takbīrat ul-Iḥrām." • Raising both hands with palms facing outwards. The hands should reach the ears each time the takbīr is recited.
Qiyām	• Placing the arms right near the knees while keeping the fingers together. • For men: keeping a distance of at least 3 fingers and upto one hand between the feet. • For women: keeping their feet together. • Looking towards the place of sajdah. • Realizing that one is standing in front of his/her Master and feeling humble.
Qirāʾah/ Dhikr	• Reciting "Aʿūdhu bil-lāhi min ash-Shayṭānir-rajīm" in a whisper before commencing Sūrah al-Fātiḥah in the first rakʿah. • Reciting Sūrah al-Qadr in the 1st rakʿah and Sūrah al-Ikhlāṣ in the 2nd rakʿah as the second sūrah of the daily obligatory prayers. • Reciting "Kadhālikallāhu Rabbī" at least once after reciting Sūrah al-Ikhlāṣ. • Reciting Sūrah al-Ikhlāṣ in either the 1st or 2nd rakʿah is highly preferred. Omitting the recitation of Sūrah al-Ikhlāṣ in the daily prayer is not recommended. • Reciting ṣalawāt after the qirāʾah.

COMPONENT	RECOMMENDED ACTIONS
Rukūʿ	• Reciting "Allāhu Akbar" before going to rukūʿ. • For men: spreading their fingers apart and placing their hands on their knees. • For women: keeping their hands on their thighs. • Keeping eyes in between the feet. • Stretching the neck in the state of rukūʿ. • Reciting the dhikr of rukūʿ three or more times. • Reciting ṣalawāt after the dhikr. • Reciting "Samiʿal-lāhu liman ḥamidah" after standing up from rukūʿ and before going into sajdah.
Sajdah	• Saying "Allāhu Akbar" (while sitting straight before going into sajdah), raising the hands for takbīr. • Putting the hands on the ground first. • Putting the entire forehead on the ground. • Placing all the fingers, including the thumbs, next to each other near the ears. • Reciting the dhikr of sajdah three or more times. • Reciting ṣalawāt after the dhikr. • Saying takbīr after rising up from first sajdah and sitting still. • Saying "Astaghfirul-lāha rabbī wa atūbu ilayh" between sajdahs. • Saying takbīr while sitting before going to second sajdah. • Making duʿā for your sustenance, health, and hereafter in sajdah, especially in the last sajdah of the prayer. • Doing tawarruk: Sitting in a special posture, between and after sajdah (i.e, to sit on your left thigh, putting the top of your right foot on the base of the left foot). • Saying "Biḥawlil-lāhi wa quwwatihi aqumu wa aqʿud" while standing up from the state of sajdah.
Tashahhud	• Saying "Alḥamdulillāh" before stating the tashahhud. • Looking towards your lap. • Putting your hands on youth thighs with the fingers next to each other in closed form.
Salām	• Doing tawarruk: sitting in a special position (discussed in sajdah). • Reciting the first phrase of the salam. "As-salāmu ʿalayka ayyuhan-nabīyyu wa raḥmatul-lāhi wa barakātuh." • Saying takbīr three times after salām.

Ta'qībāt aṣ-Ṣalāh

Recommended supplications (du'ās) to be recited after the wājib ṣalāt

FAJR

Bismillāhi	بِسْمِ اللهِ
Wa ṣallallāhu 'alā Muḥammadin-wa ālih	وَصَلَّى اللهُ عَلَىٰ مُحَمَّدٍ وَّآلِهِ
Wa ufawwiḍu amrī ilallāh	وَأُفَوِّضُ أَمْرِيْ إِلَى اللهِ
Innallāha baṣīrun-bil 'ibād	إِنَّ اللهَ بَصِيْرٌ بِالْعِبَادِ
Fawaqāhul-lāhu sayyi'āti mā makarū	فَوَقَاهُ اللهُ سَيِّئَاتِ مَا مَكَرُوْا
Lā ilāha illa anta subḥānaka	لَا إِلٰهَ إِلَّا أَنْتَ سُبْحَانَكَ
Innī kuntu minaẓ-ẓālimīn	إِنِّي كُنْتُ مِنَ الظَّالِمِيْنَ
Fastajabnā lahu wa najjaynāhu minal-ghamm	فَاسْتَجَبْنَا لَهُ وَنَجَّيْنَاهُ مِنَ الْغَمِّ
Wa kadhālika nunjil-mu'minīn	وَكَذٰلِكَ نُنْجِي الْمُؤْمِنِيْنَ
Ḥasbuna-llāhu wa ni'mal wakīl	حَسْبُنَا اللهُ وَنِعْمَ الْوَكِيْلُ
Fanqalabū bini'matin-minal-lāhi wa faḍl	فَانْقَلَبُوْا بِنِعْمَةٍ مِّنَ اللهِ وَفَضْلٍ
Lam yamsashum sū'	لَّمْ يَمْسَسْهُمْ سُوْءٌ
Māshā'Allāh	مَا شَاءَ اللهُ
La ḥawla wa lā quwwata illa billāh	لَا حَوْلَ وَلَا قُوَّةَ إِلَّا بِاللهِ
Māshā'Allāhu lā mā shā'an-nās	مَا شَاءَ اللهُ لَا مَا شَاءَ النَّاسُ
Māshā'Allāhu wa in karihan-nās	مَا شَاءَ اللهُ وَإِنْ كَرِهَ النَّاسُ
Ḥasbiyar-rabbu minal-marbūbīn	حَسْبِيَ الرَّبُّ مِنَ الْمَرْبُوْبِيْنَ
Ḥasbiyal-khāliqu minal-makhlūqīn	حَسْبِيَ الْخَالِقُ مِنَ الْمَخْلُوْقِيْنَ
Ḥasbiyar-rāziqu minal-marzūqīn	حَسْبِيَ الرَّازِقُ مِنَ الْمَرْزُوْقِيْنَ
Ḥasbiyal-lāhu rabbul-'ālamīn	حَسْبِيَ اللهُ رَبُّ الْعَالَمِيْنَ
Ḥasbī man huwa ḥasbī	حَسْبِيْ مَنْ هُوَ حَسْبِيْ
Ḥasbī man-lam yazal ḥasbī	حَسْبِيْ مَنْ لَمْ يَزَلْ حَسْبِي
Ḥasbī man kāna mudh kuntu lam yazal hasbī	حَسْبِيْ مَنْ كَانَ مُذْ كُنْتُ لَمْ يَزَلْ حَسْبِيْ
Ḥasbiyal-lāhu lā ilāha illa hū	حَسْبِيَ اللهُ لَا إِلٰهَ إِلَّا هُوَ
'Alayhi tawakkaltu	عَلَيْهِ تَوَكَّلْتُ
Wa huwa rabbul-'arshil-'aẓīm	وَهُوَ رَبُّ الْعَرْشِ الْعَظِيْمِ

With the name of Allah.

May Allah bless Muḥammad and his divine household.

I confide my cause unto Allah.

Surely, Allah is All-Seeing in relation to His servants,

so Allah warded off from him the evils which they plotted.

There is no god except You. Glorified are You!

Surely, I have been amongst the oppressors.

Then, We heard his prayer and saved him from his anguish,

and thus do We save the believers.

Allah is sufficient for us, and He is the best Guardian,

so, they returned with grace and favor from Allah,

and no evil touched them.

Only that which Allah wills (shall come to pass).

There is no strength nor power, except with Allah.

Only that which Allah wills shall come to pass, not that which people will.

Only that which Allah wills shall come to pass, even if people detest it.

Sufficient for me is the Nurturer against the nurtured.

Sufficient for me is the Creator against the creations.

Sufficient for me is the Sustainer against the sustained.

Sufficient for me is Allah, the Lord of the worlds.

Sufficient for me is He Who is sufficient.

Sufficient for me is He Who has always been sufficient.

Sufficient for me is He Who has existed since eternity and is still sufficient for me.

Allah suffices me. There is no god except Him.

In Him, I have I put my trust,

And he is the Lord of the supreme throne.

TAʿQĪBĀT AṢ-ṢALĀH

ẒUHR

Lā ilāhā illallahul-ʿaẓīmul-ḥalīm	لَا إِلٰهَ إِلَّا اللّٰهُ الْعَظِيْمُ الْحَلِيْمُ
Lā ilāhā illallahu rabbul -arshil-karīm	لَا إِلٰهَ إِلَّا اللّٰهُ رَبُّ الْعَرْشِ الْكَرِيـمِ
Alḥamdulillāhi rabbil-ʿālamīn	اَلْحَمْدُ لِلّٰهِ رَبِّ الْعَالَمِيْنَ
Allāhumma innī asaluka mūjibāti raḥmatik	اَللّٰهُمَّ إِنِّيْ اَسْاَلُكَ مُوْجِبَاتِ رَحْمَتِكَ
Wa ʿazāʾima maghfiratik	وَعَزَائِمَ مَغْفِرَتِكَ
Wal-ghanīmata min kulli birr	وَالْغَنِيْمَةَ مِنْ كُلِّ بِرٍّ
Was-salāmata min kulli ithm	وَالسَّلَامَةَ مِنْ كُلِّ إِثْمٍ
Allāhumma lā tadaʿ lī dhan-ban illa ghafartah	اَللّٰهُمَّ لَا تَدَعْ لِيْ ذَنْباً إِلَّا غَفَرْتَهُ
Wa lā hamman illa farrajtah	وَلَا هَمًّا إِلَّا فَرَّجْتَهُ
Wa lā suqman illa shafaytah	وَلَا سُقْماً إِلَّا شَفَيْتَهُ
Wa lā ʿayban illa satartah	وَلَا عَيْبًا إِلَّا سَتَرْتَهُ
Wa lā rizqan illa basaṭtah	وَلَا رِزْقاً إِلَّا بَسَطْتَهُ
Wa lā khawfan illa āmantah	وَلَا خَوْفاً إِلَّا آمَنْتَهُ
Wa lā sūʾan illa ṣaraftah	وَلَا سُوْءً اِلَّا صَرَفْتَهُ
Wa lā ḥājatan hiya laka riḍan-wa liya fīhā ṣalāḥun illa qaḍaytahā	وَلَا حَاجَةً هِيَ لَكَ رِضًا وَّلِيَ فِيْهَا صَلَاحٌ إِلَّا قَضَيْتَهَا
Yā arḥamar-rāḥimīn	يَا اَرْحَمَ الرَّاحِمِيْنَ
Āmīna rabbal-ʿālamīn	آمِيْنَ رَبَّ الْعَالَمِيْنَ

ʿAṢR

Astaghfirul-lāhal-ladhī lā ilāha illa hū	اَسْتَغْفِرُ اللّٰهَ الَّذِيْ لَا إِلٰهَ إِلَّا هُوَ
Al-ḥayyul qayyūm	الْحَيُّ الْقَيُّوْمُ
Ar-raḥmānur-raḥīm	الرَّحْمٰنُ الرَّحِيْمُ
Dhul-jalāli wal-ikrām	ذُو الْجَلَالِ وَالْإِكْرَامِ
Wa asaluhu an-yatūba ʿalayya	وَ اَسْاَلُهُ اَنْ يَتُوْبَ عَلَيَّ
Tawbata ʿabdin dhalīlin khāḍiʿin	تَوْبَةَ عَبْدٍ ذَلِيْلٍ خَاضِعٍ
Faqīrin bāʾisin	فَقِيْرٍ بَائِسٍ
Miskīnin mustakīnin mustajīr	مِسْكِيْنٍ مُسْتَكِيْنٍ مُسْتَجِيْرٍ
Lā yamliku linafsihi nafʿan-wa lā ḍarra	لَا يَمْلِكُ لِنَفْسِهٖ نَفْعًا وَّلَا ضَرًّا
Wa lā mawtan-wa lā ḥayātan-wa lā nushūrā	وَلَا مَوْتًا وَّلَا حَيَاةً وَّلَا نُشُوْرًا

There is no god except Allah, the Supreme, the Forbearing.

There is no god except Allah, Lord of the honorable throne.

All praise is for Allah, Lord of the worlds.

O Allah, I ask You to grant me that which will give me Your mercy,

the strength for a strong will that will allow me to attain your forgiveness

the advantage of each act of kindness,

and safeguarding from all sins.

O Allah, (please) do not leave any of my offenses except that they are forgiven,

any of my misfortunes except that they are relieved,

any of my ailments except that they are cured,

any of my faults except that they are covered,

any sustenance, except that it is increased

any fear, except that it is protected

any evil (that comes upon me), except that it is controlled

and any wish that achieves Your satisfaction and my benefit,
except that it is granted.

O the most Merciful!

Let it be so, O Lord of the worlds!

I seek forgiveness from Allah, besides whom there is no god,

the All-living, the Self-Subsisting,

the All-Compassionate, the All-Merciful,

the Lord of majesty and honor.

I ask Him to accept my repentance,

As the repentance of a slave who is submissive, humble,

poor, miserable,

despondent, dejected, seeking refuge (with Him),

not controlling for himself any harm or profit,

and not controlling death nor life, nor raising (the dead) to life.

MAGHRIB

Allāhumma innī asaluka mūjibāti raḥmatik	اَللّٰهُمَّ إِنِّى اَسْاَلُكَ مُوجِبَاتِ رَحْمَتِكَ
Wa ʿazāʾima maghfiratik	وَعَزَائِمِ مَغْفِرَتِكَ
Wan-najāta minan-nār	وَالنَّجَاةَ مِنَ النَّارِ
Wa min kulli balīyyah	وَمِنْ كُلِّ بَلِيَّةٍ
Wal-fawza bil-jannah	وَالْفَوْزَ بِالْجَنَّةِ
War-riḍwāni fī dāris-salām	وَالرِّضْوَانِ فِىْ دَارِ السَّلَامِ
Wa jawāri nabīyyika Muḥammadin ʿalayhi wa ālihis-salām	وَجِوَارِ نَبِيِّكَ مُحَمَّدٍ عَلَيْهِ وَآلِهِ السَّلَامُ
Allāhumma mā binā min niʿmatin famink	اَللّٰهُمَّ مَا بِنَا مِنْ نِعْمَةٍ فَمِنْكَ
Lā ilāha illa ant	لَا إِلٰهَ إِلَّا اَنْتَ
Astaghfiruka wa atūbu ilayk	اَسْتَغْفِرُكَ وَ اَتُوْبُ إِلَيْكَ

ʿISHĀʾ

Allāhumma innahu laysa lī ʿilmun bimawāḍiʿi rizqī	اَللّٰهُمَّ إِنَّهُ لَيْسَ لِىْ عِلْمٌ بِمَوْضِعِ رِزْقِىْ
Wa innamā aṭlubuhu bikhaṭarātin takhṭuru ʿalā qalbī	وَإِنَّمَا اَطْلُبُهُ بِخَطَرَاتٍ تَخْطُرُ عَلٰى قَلْبِىْ
Fa ajulu fī ṭalabihil-buldān	فَاَجُوْلُ فِىْ طَلَبِهِ الْبُلْدَانَ
Fa anā fīmā anā ṭālibun kal-ḥayrān	فَاَنَا فِيْمَا اَنَا طَالِبٌ كَالْحَيْرَانِ
Lā adrī afī sahlin huwa am fī jabal	لَا اَدْرِى اَفِىْ سَهْلٍ هُوَ اَمْ فِىْ جَبَلٍ
Am fī arḍin am fī samāʾ	اَمْ فِىْ اَرْضٍ اَمْ فِىْ سَمَاءٍ
Am fī barrin am fī baḥr	اَمْ فِى بَرٍّ اَمْ فِى بَحْرٍ
Wa ʿalā yaday man	وَعَلٰى يَدَىْ مَنْ
Wa min qibali man	وَمِنْ قِبَلِ مَنْ
Wa qad ʿalimtu anna ʿilmahu ʿindak	وَقَدْ عَلِمْتُ اَنَّ عِلْمَهُ عِنْدَكَ
Wa asbābahu biyadik	وَ اَسْبَابَهُ بِيَدِكَ
Wa antal-ladhī taqsimuhu bilutfik	وَ اَنْتَ الَّذِى تَقْسِمُهُ بِلُطْفِكَ
Wa tusabbibuhu biraḥmatik	وَتُسَبِّبُهُ بِرَحْمَتِكَ
Allāhumma faṣalli ʿalā Muḥammadin-wa ālih	اَللّٰهُمَّ فَصَلِّ عَلٰى مُحَمَّدٍ وَآلِهِ
Waj-ʿal yā rabbi rizqaka lī wāsiʿā	وَاجْعَلْ يَا رَبِّ رِزْقَكَ لِىْ وَاسِعًا
Wa maṭlabahu sahlā	وَمَطْلَبَهُ سَهْلًا
Wa maʾkhadhahu qarībā	وَمَاْخَذَهُ قَرِيْبًا
Wa lā tuʿanninī biṭalabi mā lam tuqaddir lī fīhi rizqā	وَلَا تُعَنِّنِى بِطَلَبِ مَا لَمْ تُقَدِّرْ لِىْ فِيْهِ رِزْقًا
Fa innaka ghanīyyun ʿan ʿadhābī	فَإِنَّكَ غَنِىٌّ عَنْ عَذَابِىْ
Wa anā faqīrun ilā raḥmatik	وَ اَنَا فَقِيْرٌ إِلٰى رَحْمَتِكَ
Faṣalli ʿalā Muḥammadin-wa ālih	فَصَلِّ عَلٰى مُحَمَّدٍ وَّآلِهِ
Wa jud ʿalā ʿabdika bifaḍlik	وَجُدْ عَلٰى عَبْدِكَ بِفَضْلِكَ
Innaka dhū faḍlil-ʿaẓīm	إِنَّكَ ذُوْ فَضْلِ الْعَظِيْمِ

O Allah! I beseech You for the motives of Your mercy,
the determining causes of Your forgiveness,
safety from the Hellfire,
and from all misfortunes,
the success of Paradise,
contentment in the Peaceful Abode,
and (being in) the vicinity of Your Prophet Muḥammad — peace be upon him and his Divine Household.
O Allah, You are certainly the source of each and every favor that covers us.
There is no god save You.
I seek Your forgiveness and repent to You.

O Allah! I surely lack knowledge about the place of my sustenance;
rather, I am seeking it according to the ideas that enter my heart.
Therefore, I wander in the different countries searching for it.
By doing so, I am as confused as the confounded,
since I do not know whether my sustenance lies in a plain, on a mountain,
In the earth or in the skies,
In the lands or in seas,
and at whose hands,
or who the source of it is.
I know that you have full knowledge of all this,
And its cause is through Your hands
and it is You Who distributes it out of Your compassion
and cause it by Your mercy.
O Allah, please send blessings to Muhammad and his Household
and make, O Lord, Your sustenance that is provided to me expansive,
my seeking for it easy for me,
and its source nearby.
Please, do not fatigue me by seeking that which You have not decided for me to have,
because You are certainly in no need for tormenting me
while I am in full need for Your mercy.
(Please) Send blessings upon Muhammad and his Household
and confer liberally upon me, Your slave, out of Your graciousness.
Surely, you are the Lord of supreme grace.

Imām aṣ-Ṣādiq (ʿa) has said:

"When a man completes his ṣalāh with the Prostration of Thanks, Allah lifts the veil between the angels and man and addresses them, 'O angels, look at My creature who has performed his duty to Me and fulfilled his promise to Me and has then prostrated in gratitude to Me for all the blessings that I have bestowed on him. O angels, what shall I give him?' They respond, 'O God, Your mercy.' He asks, 'What else?' They reply, "O God, Your Heaven.' Again, He asks, 'What else?' They say, 'Fulfill his needs and grant him his wishes.' Allah continues to repeat the question and the angels respond until they are unable to provide further reply and say that they do not know. Then, Allah says, 'I, too, must thank him as he has done, grant him prosperity by My grace, and treat him with My great mercy on the Day of Judgment.'"

(*Thawāb al-Aʿmāl wa ʿIqāb al-Aʿmāl*, P. 295)